HEINEMANN G
BEGINN

BETSY PENNINK

This is San Francisco

HEINEMANN

HEINEMANN GUIDED READERS
BEGINNER LEVEL

Series Editor: John Milne

The Heinemann Guided Readers provide a choice of enjoyable reading material for learners of English. The Series is published at five levels – Starter, Beginner, Elementary, Intermediate and Upper. At **Beginner Level**, the control of content and language has the following main features:

Information Control
The stories are written in a fluent and pleasing style with straightforward plots and a restricted number of main characters. The cultural background is made explicit through both words and illustrations. Information which is vital to the story is clearly presented and repeated where necessary.

Structure Control
Special care is taken with sentence length. Most sentences contain only one clause, though compound sentences are used occasionally with the clauses joined by the conjunctions 'and', 'but', and 'or'. The use of these compound sentences gives the text balance and rhythm. The use of Past Simple and Past Continuous Tenses is permitted since these are the basic tenses used in narration and students must become familiar with these as they continue to extend and develop their reading ability.

Vocabulary Control
At **Beginner Level** there is a controlled vocabulary of approximately 600 basic words, so that students with a basic knowledge of English will be able to read with understanding and enjoyment. Help is also given in the form of vivid illustrations which are closely related to the text.

For further information on the full selection of Readers at all five levels in the series, please refer to the Heinemann Guided Readers catalogue.

CONTENTS

	Introduction	4
1	History of San Francisco	5
2	Getting to Know San Francisco	11
3	Things to See and Do	19
4	Glossary of American/British English	30
5	Information and Advice	31

INTRODUCTION

San Francisco is an important city on the west coast of the United States of America. It is not a very large city. Only 679 000 people live in San Francisco.

But San Francisco is the financial center of western America. It is also a center for music and art. And it is a city for tourists. Three and a half million people visit San Francisco every year.

San Francisco is an international city. People from many countries live there. Let us look at this interesting city.

San Francisco – a view over the bay

1 HISTORY of SAN FRANCISCO

The Spanish in California

San Francisco and California are Spanish names. In 1520, the Spanish army took Mexico, in North America. After that, Spanish explorers looked for more land. They sailed north along the western coast of North America. They called the land along the coast California.

Many years later, Spanish soldiers and monks went together into California. The monks were religious teachers, or missionaries. Between 1769 and 1823, monks built twenty-one missions along the coast of California. They taught their religion to American Indians at these missions.

Near each mission, soldiers built a military post. The soldiers protected the mission and protected the land too.

Spanish monks at a mission in California

San Francisco and its Bay

The Mission of San Francisco de Asis

Spanish ships sailed into some beautiful bays on the California coast. These bays made very good harbors. But the sailors did not find the biggest bay of all. The opening to this bay was very small, and it was often hidden by fog. The Spanish sailors did not see it.

In 1769, some Spanish soldiers found the bay. The bay was separated from the ocean by a peninsula – a long piece of land. The soldiers returned to their post and described the bay.

Seven years later, Spanish soldiers and monks came to the bay. They built a military post on the peninsula. They also built the Mission of San Francisco de Asis. San Francisco, or Saint Francis, is a saint in the Roman Catholic religion.

From Spain to Mexico to America

For seventy years, San Francisco was a small village. But many things were changing in North America.

In 1776, the United States of America became a free country. In 1821, the Mexicans defeated the Spanish, and Mexico became a free country. California was governed by Mexico.

From 1846 to 1848, there was a war between the United States and Mexico. After the war, Mexico gave California to the United States. At this time, about 800 people were living in San Francisco.

In 1850, California became the thirty-first state of the United States of America.

San Francisco in 1848

Gold!

Looking for gold

In 1848, gold was discovered in the hills near San Francisco. After that, San Francisco changed completely.

In 1849, men came to San Francisco from all over the world. They were called 'Forty-Niners' and they were looking for gold. Some were from the United States. Some came from South America, Australia and China. Many came by land, but others came by sea. More than 500 ships sailed into San Francisco Bay through the narrow entrance – the Golden Gate. The men left the ships in the Bay and hurried into the mountains.

About 80 000 men came to California in the Gold Rush. Some of these 'Forty-Niners' found gold and became very rich. But most of them found nothing.

The Wild City

The population of San Francisco grew to 35 000 in two years. All kinds of people lived there. Millionaires built beautiful, big houses on Nob Hill. Other people lived in small, bad houses.

There were not many laws. San Francisco was a wild city. People drank a lot of whiskey and smoked opium. They gambled and lost their money. There were dangerous groups of bad men, or 'hoodlums'. The hoodlums robbed and killed many people.

But San Francisco became larger and larger. It became the financial center of the western United States. Soon there was a railroad all the way from the eastern United States to San Francisco. The city also had a busy harbor. Ships came across the Pacific Ocean from many countries – especially China.

The Railroad – New York to San Francisco

The Earthquake

On 18 April 1906, San Francisco was shaken by a terrible earthquake. Soon large fires were burning all over the city. The fires burned for three days. One third of all the buildings were destroyed and hundreds of people were killed. But all the bad parts of the city were gone!

The San Franciscans built their city again very quickly. Now San Francisco has old and new buildings. It is bigger and more beautiful. It is also healthier and safer.

San Francisco after the Earthquake in 1906

2 GETTING to KNOW SAN FRANCISCO

The Peninsula and the Hills

San Francisco is a special city for several reasons. Here is one: the city has water on three sides. On the west is the Pacific Ocean. On the east is San Francisco Bay. On the north, between the Ocean and the Bay, is the Golden Gate.

The Golden Gate is the entrance to the Bay. At one point it is only a mile (1.6 km) wide. Here, the famous Golden Gate Bridge goes from San Francisco to Marin County on the other side.

San Francisco's other bridge goes across the Bay to Oakland, a smaller city. It is called the San Francisco-Oakland Bay Bridge, or 'the Bay Bridge'.

Oakland Bay Bridge

Cars on Lombard Street – one of San Francisco's hills

San Francisco is built on many hills. There are forty! Some of the hills are very high and very steep. Most of the streets go north and south, or east and west. The streets go up and down the hills. A few streets go through the hills. At the top of many hills there are wonderful views of the city and the water around it.

The Climate

San Francisco has a special climate. It is never very hot or very cold. In December, the average temperature is 52.5°F (11.4°C). In July, it is 58.8°F (15°C).

The weather can change several times during one day. Often it is foggy, especially in the morning. Then the sun shines. San Franciscans always have jackets with them. Only ten miles (16 km) outside San Francisco, the temperature can go over 100°F (36.6°C) in summer!

Getting Around in San Francisco

It is easy to see San Francisco. Many of the interesting places are near each other. Look at the map on pages 14 and 15. Can you find these two streets: Market Street and Van Ness Avenue? The most important part of San Francisco is between these two streets and the water.

Visitors walk along the streets of San Francisco. But they can get around the city in many other ways.

Buses go all over the city. Each ride – long or short – costs the same. But you must have the right coins. Bus drivers do not make change. You can continue your ride on a different bus. Ask the first bus driver for a transfer. A transfer is a free ticket for the second bus. You can use it any time in the next two hours.

San Francisco also has streetcars. They begin on Market Street. Sometimes trains run under Market Street instead of the streetcars. This subway is called the Muni Metro.

There are also many taxis in San Francisco.

The Muni Metro

SAN F
NAPA VALLEY
MARIN COUNTY
RICHMOND-SAN RAPHAEL BRIDGE
TIBURON
SAUSALITO
GOLDEN GATE TOLL BRIDGE
BERKELEY
OAKLAND
METROPOLITAN OAKLAND INTERNATIONAL AIRPORT
GOLDEN GATE PARK
SAN FRANCISCO INTERNATIONAL AIRPORT
SAN MATEO TOLL BRIDGE
SAN FRANCISCO
GOLDEN GATE BRIDGE
GOLDEN GATE BOULEVARD
LINCOLN BOULEVARD
PARK PRESIDIO BLVD
N
W
E
S
8
CALIFORNIA STREET
LINCOLN PARK
GEARY BOULEVARD
STAVYAN STREET
MASONIC AVENUE
SEAL ROCK
BALBOA BOULEVARD
FULTON STREET
M.H. DE YOUNG MEMORIAL MUSEUM
GOLDEN GATE PARK
ASIAN ART MUSEUM
7
LINCOLN WAY
GREAT HIGHWAY
SUNSET BOULEVARD
NOREGA STREET
NINETEENTH AVENUE
TWIN PEAKS
PACIFIC OCEAN
TARAVAL STREET
VICENTE STREET
PORTOLA DRIVE
SAN FRANCISCO ZOO
SLOAT BOULEVARD
MONTERE
LAKE MERCED

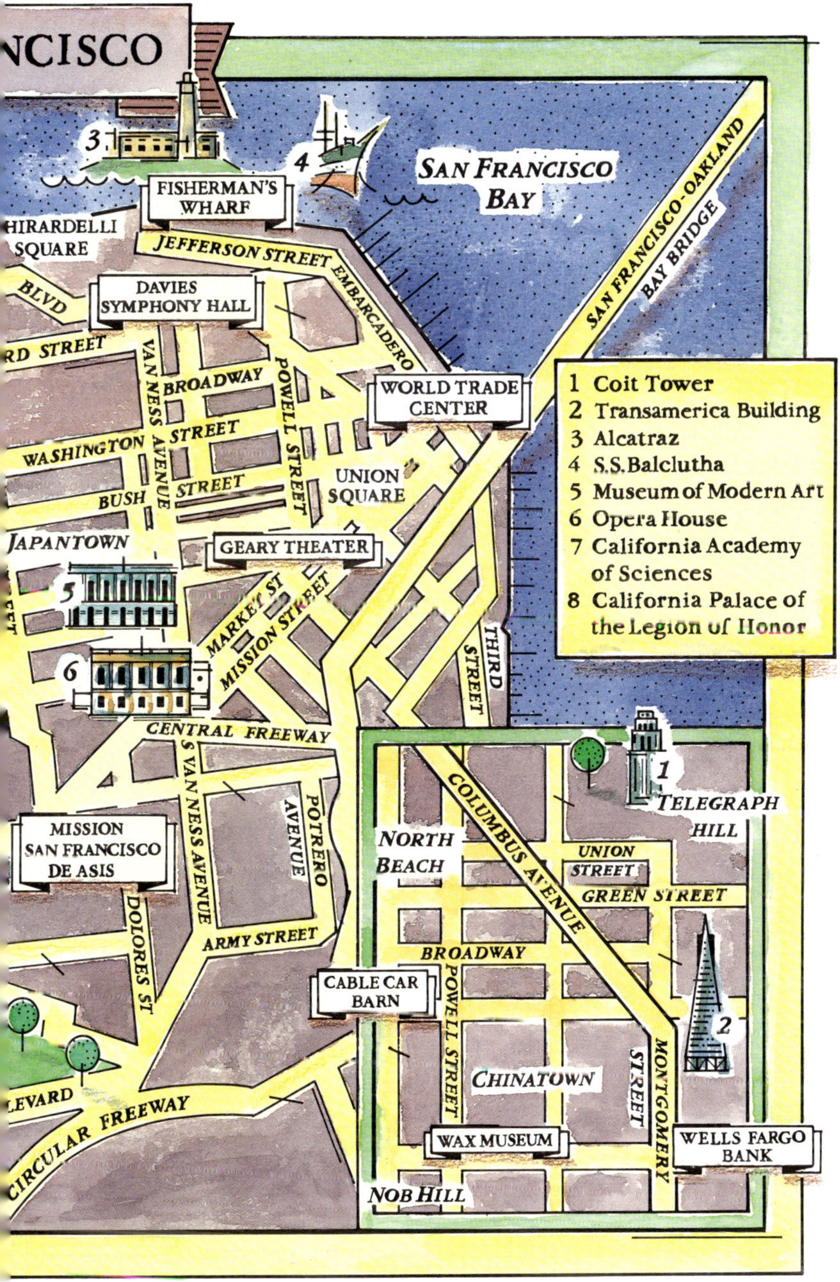
NCISCO
SAN FRANCISCO BAY
3
4
FISHERMAN'S WHARF
HIRARDELLI SQUARE
JEFFERSON STREET
EMBARCADERO
SAN FRANCISCO-OAKLAND BAY BRIDGE
BLVD
DAVIES SYMPHONY HALL
RD STREET
VAN NESS AVENUE
BROADWAY
POWELL STREET
WORLD TRADE CENTER
WASHINGTON STREET
BUSH STREET
UNION SQUARE
JAPANTOWN
GEARY THEATER
5
MARKET ST
MISSION STREET
6
THIRD STREET
CENTRAL FREEWAY
S VAN NESS AVENUE
POTRERO AVENUE
MISSION SAN FRANCISCO DE ASIS
DOLORES ST
ARMY STREET
CABLE CAR BARN
LEVARD
CIRCULAR FREEWAY
1 Coit Tower
2 Transamerica Building
3 Alcatraz
4 S.S.Balclutha
5 Museum of Modern Art
6 Opera House
7 California Academy of Sciences
8 California Palace of the Legion of Honor
1
TELEGRAPH HILL
NORTH BEACH
COLUMBUS AVENUE
UNION STREET
GREEN STREET
BROADWAY
POWELL STREET
2
CHINATOWN
STREET
MONTGOMERY
WAX MUSEUM
WELLS FARGO BANK
NOB HILL

The Cable Cars

A cable car

San Francisco is famous for its cable cars. Its first cable car was made in 1873 by Andrew Hallidie, an engineer. At that time, streetcars were pulled up and down the hills by horses. Sometimes a horse fell. Then all the horses and the streetcar rolled down the hill. Hallidie wanted a streetcar without horses.

The cable cars are pulled by a heavy wire rope – a cable – under the street. The cable always moves at the same speed: 9.5 miles (15.2 km) per hour. There are three cable car lines in the city.

The cable cars are old-fashioned, but everyone loves them. Visitors always ride on them. And San Franciscans often go to work by cable car!

Neighborhoods

Today there are 82 000 Chinese people in San Francisco. This is the largest group of Chinese outside Asia. Many of these Chinese people live in *Chinatown*.

The first Chinese came to San Francisco in the Gold Rush. Thousands more came between 1860 and 1870. They built the last part of the railroad to San Francisco.

The main street of Chinatown is *Grant Avenue*. Many of the buildings look Chinese. There are excellent restaurants. The shops sell many Chinese things – from vegetables to beautiful Chinese art.

There is an interesting Wax Museum on Grant Avenue. It shows the history of Chinatown.

Chinatown

North Beach begins north of Chinatown. Most of the people in North Beach are Italian. There are many little Italian shops, cafés and restaurants here. Every October there is an Italian celebration in *Washington Square*. It tells the story of Christopher Columbus. He discovered America in 1492.

Columbus Avenue and *Broadway* are in North Beach. But they are very different from the Italian part. Columbus Avenue has interesting bookshops. Artists and writers often sit and talk in cafés nearby. Broadway has nightclubs.

Japantown is in the west of San Francisco. Many Japanese people live there. The Japan Center was built in Japantown in 1968. It has a modern Japanese hotel, gardens, restaurants, bath-houses and shops.

Broadway at night

3 THINGS to SEE and DO

Victorian houses and skyscrapers behind them

Victorian Houses and Skyscrapers

On some streets in San Francisco there are interesting old houses. They were built before 1906 in the Victorian style. The fronts of these houses have a lot of decoration. In San Francisco the Victorian houses are narrow. They have bay windows – with glass on three sides. San Franciscans paint their Victorian houses in bright colors.

People admire San Francisco's modern buildings too. An example is the Transamerica Building. It was built in 1972 on *Montgomery Street*, the main street of the financial center. It has the shape of a tall pyramid. Other tall buildings – skyscrapers – are nearby.

Fisherman's Wharf

Every morning, more than 150 fishing boats go out from San Francisco. They leave from a pier on the waterfront. This part of the waterfront – from Hyde Street to Powell Street – is called *Fisherman's Wharf*.

Visitors walk beside the water there. They watch street artists and they buy many things in the shops. They visit an old sailing ship, the *Balclutha*, at one of the piers.

Fishing boats at Fisherman's Wharf

On *Jefferson Street* there are many seafood restaurants. But visitors can also eat crabs from the stalls on the sidewalk. The crabs are cooked in big pots and visitors eat them with some of San Francisco's famous white bread.

A man cooking crabs

Boat Rides

The rocky island called Alcatraz

In San Francisco Bay, there is a rocky island. It is called *Alcatraz*. In 1934, a prison was built there for very dangerous prisoners. The prisoners could not escape alive. The water around Alcatraz is cold and it pulls swimmers out to sea.

In 1962, three prisoners disappeared from Alcatraz. Did they escape? Nobody knows. The next year, the prison was closed.

Today there is a very interesting tour of Alcatraz. Guides take people through the prison. Visitors can go inside one of the small rooms or cells. The boats for Alcatraz leave from Fisherman's Wharf.

Three other boat rides take visitors around San Francisco Bay. The boats go under both bridges and very close to Alcatraz.

Telegraph Hill and Nob Hill

One of the best views of the city and the Bay is from *Coit Tower* on *Telegraph Hill*.

As a girl, Lillie Coit liked firemen. She rode to fires on their fire engines. After her death, the city was given some of her money. Coit Tower was built in 1933.

Most of the millionaires' homes on *Nob Hill* were destroyed in the earthquake of 1906. But there are expensive buildings on Nob Hill today. Four of the best hotels are also there.

The *Cable Car Barn* is on Washington Street on Nob Hill. Visitors can watch the big wheels in the barn. The wheels turn and move the cables for the cable cars.

Coit Tower

Parks and Museums

The Japanese Tea Garden

Golden Gate Park is San Francisco's most important park. In 1868, it was only sand. Now it has over a million trees. It has a golf course. It has a Japanese Tea Garden with small bridges over pools of water.

There are two important art museums in Golden Gate Park. The *M.H. De Young Memorial Museum* often has famous exhibitions. The *Asian Art Museum* has over 10 000 pieces of Oriental art.

The *California Academy of Sciences* is in the same part of the park. This well-known science museum has an aquarium with unusual fish.

Lincoln Park is north of Golden Gate Park. It is on the ocean. From the cliffs you can see *Seal Rock*. Seals and sea-lions live there. Lincoln Park also has an art museum, the *California Palace of the Legion of Honor*.

Visitors admire the Golden Gate Bridge. There is a very good view of it from the *Golden Gate Promenade*.

Golden Gate Bridge

This walk begins under the Golden Gate Bridge at Fort Point. It goes along the water to Fisherman's Wharf.

The west coast of the San Franciscan peninsula is called *Ocean Beach*. At the south end of Ocean Beach is the *San Francisco Zoo*. It is famous for its very small hippopotamuses.

Another art museum in San Francisco is the *Museum of Modern Art* on Van Ness Avenue.

Do you like the history of the Wild West? Go to the History Room at the *Wells Fargo Bank* on Montgomery Street. There you can see an old stagecoach. For forty years after the Gold Rush, these coaches carried people, letters and gold in the West. The driver and the guard rode on top of the stagecoach. The guard had a gun. He protected the stagecoach against robbers.

A visit to the *Mission San Francisco de Asis* is interesting too. This old church is also called Mission Dolores. It is south of Market Street on Dolores Street. Visitors can see the beautiful Indian designs on the ceiling.

Shopping

Shopping in San Francisco is exciting. The most important shopping area is around *Union Square*. All the large department stores are there. *I. Magnin* and *Macy's* are examples. *Post Street* has shops for china, silver and glass. One of these is *Gump's*, a famous old store.

The flower stalls in this area are famous too. There is one on every street corner!

The Victorian houses on *Union Street* are now unusual shops. Many of them sell antiques.

There is good shopping on Fisherman's Wharf. At *Ghirardelli Square* and *The Cannery* you can buy many things. Years ago, Ghirardelli Square was a chocolate factory and The Cannery was a fruit canning factory. *Pier 39* nearby has over a hundred good shops.

Ghiradelli Square

Restaurants and Entertainment

The first San Franciscans ate Spanish food. Today, San Franciscans can eat food from more than fifty countries. There is an American restaurant with thirty-eight different kinds of hamburgers. One hamburger has chocolate sauce on it!

There is excellent entertainment in San Francisco. For example, the famous Opera Company and Ballet Company perform at the *Opera House* on Van Ness Avenue. The Symphony Orchestra gives concerts at the *Davies Symphony Hall*.

There are both large and small theaters in San Francisco. A well-known group of actors – the American Conservatory Theater – is at the *Geary Theater* on Geary Street.

The Davies Symphony Hall

The Wine Country

Napa Valley – a vineyard

Spanish monks planted the first grape vines in California. They made wine for their churches from the grapes. Today, California wine is very well-known.

The most famous area for wine in California is the *Napa Valley*. It is 55 miles (88.5 km) north of San Francisco.

About sixty wineries – wine companies – grow grapes in the Napa Valley. Visitors can see the grape vines from the road.

Visitors are welcome at the wineries. Guides take the visitors through the buildings. They explain about wine-making. They describe the different kinds of wine. Afterwards, visitors can taste some of the wine.

Napa Valley – a wine cellar

The Bay Area

The land all around San Francisco Bay is called the Bay Area. There is a lot to see in this area.

Marin County is across the Golden Gate Bridge. Some people live in Marin County and work in San Francisco. They like the sunshine in Marin County and they want to live on the Bay. Their favorite villages are *Tiburon* and *Sausalito*. Artists and fishermen live in Sausalito too.

Not everyone goes from San Francisco to Marin County by car. Many people go by ferry across the Bay. Another ferry takes visitors to *Angel Island* in the Bay. The island is a large park. Many deer and other animals live there. Visitors fish and have picnics on this quiet island.

Berkeley and *Oakland* are small cities on the east side of the Bay. Berkeley is famous for its university. Oakland's waterfront is now the busiest port in the Bay Area.

The BART underground train connects the city with Berkeley and Oakland.

Sausalito in Marin Country

Muir Woods is another lovely park in Marin County. It is a forest of California redwood trees. Some are 1200 years old. They are more than 300 feet (91m) high. California redwood trees are the tallest trees in the world.

Redwood trees – the tallest trees in the world

4 GLOSSARY of AMERICAN/ BRITISH ENGLISH

Some words are spelt differently in American and British English. These are a few of them.

American English	*British English*
center	centre
color	colour
favorite	favourite
harbor	harbour
neighborhood	neighbourhood
theater	theatre
whiskey	whisky

Other words are different in American and British English.

American English	*British English*
make change	give change
railroad	railway
sailboat	sailing-boat
sidewalk	pavement
subway	underground/tube
mail	post

5 INFORMATION and ADVICE

Perhaps you will visit San Francisco one day. Have a good time! Here is some advice.

Bring some warm clothes and comfortable shoes. Get a good map of the city. The *Regional Transit Guide* has bus, streetcar and cable car routes.

General Information

Tourist Offices

San Francisco Convention and Visitors' Bureau
Visitor Information Center
Hallidie Plaza
Powell and Market Street

or write to:
P.O. Box 6977
San Francisco, CA 94101
Telephone (415) 391–2000

Visitor Information Center
Redwood Empire Association
785 Market
San Francisco, CA 94105
Telephone (415) 543–8338

Transport Information

The MUNI (San Francisco Municipal Railway)
Telephone (415) 673–6864 (day or night)

BART (Bay Area Rapid Transit System)
Telephone (415) 788–2278

Golden Gate Transit (information on buses and ferries to Marin County)
Telephone (415) 332–6600

Useful Phone Numbers

The Weather (415) 767–8900
The Time (415) 936–1212
Emergency:
  Police, Fire, Ambulance
  431–2800
  or 'O' for Operator or 911

Heinemann International
A division of Heinemann Publishers (Oxford) Ltd
Halley Court, Jordan Hill, Oxford OX2 8EJ

OXFORD LONDON EDINBURGH
MADRID ATHENS BOLOGNA PARIS
MELBOURNE SYDNEY AUCKLAND SINGAPORE TOKYO
IBADAN NAIROBI HARARE GABORONE
PORTSMOUTH (NH)

ISBN 0 435 27179 2

© Betsy Pennink 1982, 1992
First published 1982
Reprinted three times
This edition published 1992

All rights reserved; no part of this publication may be
reproduced, stored in a retrieval system, or transmitted, in any
form or by any means, electronic, mechanical, photocopying,
recording or otherwise, without the prior written permission of
the Publishers.

Acknowledgements
The authors and publishers would like to thank the following for permission to
reproduce their photographs and artwork: Michael Boyd p16; Greg Evans Photo
Library p11, p17, p20 (t), p27 (b); Mary Evans Picture Library p8; Robert Harding
Picture Library p6; The Hulton Picture Company p7, p10; Image Bank p22; Image
Bank/Luis Castaneda p23; Image Bank/Gerard Champlong p12; Image Bank/Niki
Mareschal p25; Image Bank/Steve Proehl p27 (t); Image Bank/Harald Sund p29;
Peter Newark's Western Americana p5; The Photographers' Library p21;
Quadrant/Wiseman/R. Gaz p13; Tony Stone Photo Library p19, p24; Tony Stone
Photo Library/Roy Giles p20 (b); Syndication International/Library of Congress p9;
World Pictures/Feature-Pix Colour Library p28; Zefa p4, p18; Zefa/K. Goebel p26.

Typography by Adrian Hodgkins
Cover by Christina Brimage and Threefold Design
Map by Sue Potter
Typeset in 12/16 pt Goudy
by Joshua Associates Ltd, Oxford
Printed and bound in Spain

92 93 94 95 96 97 10 9 8 7 6 5 4 3 2 1